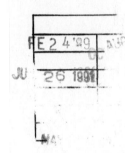

THE GREAT BOOK OF

HELICOPTERS

THE GREAT BOOK OF

HELICOPTERS

Text by David White

Rourke Enterprises, Inc.
Vero Beach, FL 32964

Library of Congress Cataloging-in-Publication Data

White, David, 1952–
  Helicopters/David White.
    p.   cm.—(The great book of—)
    Includes index.
    Summary: Describes the uses, types, principles of flying, and historical
development of the helicopter.
    ISBN 0-86592-451-1
    1. Helicopters—Juvenile literature.   [1. Helicopters.]
I. Title.   II. Series: White, David, 1952–   Great book of—.
TL716.W47   1988
629.133'352—dc19   87-36906
                                               CIP
                                               AC

Contents

How Does a Helicopter Fly?

Although it flies differently, a helicopter works on the same principle as an airplane. As the rotors turn, air flows around them in the same way that it flows around the wings of an airplane taking off. This lifts the helicopter off the ground.

A helicopter cannot fly as fast as an airplane. Unequal forces on the turning blades of the helicopter make them vibrate. These unequal forces, known as "disymmetry of lift," could turn a helicopter over in the early days.

To solve this problem, Juan de la Cierva invented the flapping hinge to connect the blades to the helicopter. This allowed the blades to move more freely and reduced vibration. Another solution was to have two rotors, one on top of the other, turning in different directions. This ensured that the helicopter stayed upright.

But the best idea came from Igor Sikorsky. He put a small rotor, at right angles to the main rotor, on the tail of the helicopter. This stopped the helicopter from twisting in flight.

A helicopter hovers or moves vertically by pushing air down with its rotor.

The rotor blades flex upwards as they move forwards.

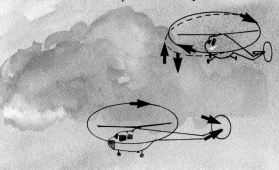

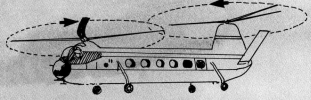

The twist of the large rotor is compensated by a small rotor near the tail.

Bristol 173 — a helicopter balanced by having two large rotors which rotate in opposite directions.

What is the difference between a helicopter and a gyrocopter?

It is easy to confuse a helicopter with a gyrocopter. They look the same, but they work quite differently.

Gyrocopters have an engine in the front, just like an airplane. Their rotor blades are not connected to an engine. Instead, they are turned by the air when the gyrocopter moves forward.

This means that gyrocopters cannot take off and land vertically, as helicopters can. They need a short strip or runway to fly from.

However, in many ways they are safer than helicopters. If their engines fail, their rotor blades continue to turn. They can therefore land safely.

In spite of this, gyrocopters have never been given important jobs to do. Mostly, they are used for fun. One made an appearance in a James Bond film.

The Invention of the Helicopter

The first helicopters were toys. Many centuries ago children in China played with a simple mechanism which launched a four-bladed rotor into the air. You can still buy toys like this today.

In the 16th century Leonardo da Vinci, the Italian painter and inventor, designed a *helixpteron* (which means "spiral wing") to lift a man off the ground. But we do not know if he ever built one.

There were many experiments with small vertical flying devices in the 18th century. All of these used steam engines, which were too heavy. However, the invention of the internal combustion engine made vertical human flight a real possibility.

Early manned helicopters were very unstable. Some turned over in mid-air. This problem was partly solved by Spanish inventor, Juan de la Cierva. He designed a machine, which he called an autogiro, that was almost impossible to turn over.

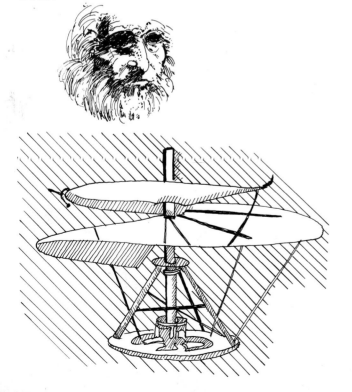

The "father of the helicopter," however, was Igor Sikorsky, a Russian who emigrated to America. He built his first helicopter in 1909, but couldn't get it off the ground. It was not until 30 years later that his VS-300 helicopter rose into the air. This set a record by staying in the air for more than one and a half hours. This was the first modern helicopter.

Some important dates

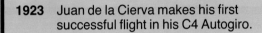

1907 Paul Cornu, a Frenchman, becomes the first man to rise vertically in a powered flying machine. The flight lasted just 20 seconds, and the helicopter rose only six feet in the air.

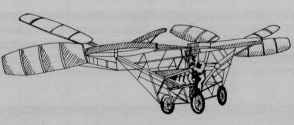

1923 Juan de la Cierva makes his first successful flight in his C4 Autogiro.

1924 The Marquis di Pescara flies a helicopter which stays up for 10 minutes and 10 seconds, and covers a distance of 448 feet in a straight line. This is the first helicopter to move forwards as well as upwards.

1936 The first practical helicopter in history, the Focke-Achgelis Fw 61, is built and flown in Germany. However, it has two rotors rather than one to help it fly.

1940 Igor Sikorsky makes the first successful flight with a single rotor helicopter in America, the VS-300. This is the forerunner of the modern helicopter.

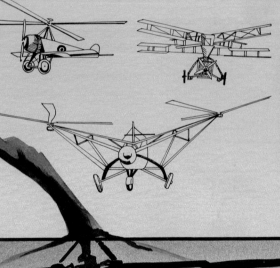

At the Controls

Flying a helicopter is far more difficult than flying an airplane. The pilot of a helicopter needs good coordination to be able to operate the controls correctly.

The difficulty is that a helicopter has two flying controls, while the airplane has only one. These are the *collective pitch lever* and the *cyclic pitch control stick*. One controls vertical flight, and the other controls horizontal flight.

By operating the collective pitch lever, the pilot can alter the pitch, or angle, of all the rotor blades. This increases or decreases lift, causing the helicopter to ascend or descend.

By operating the cyclic pitch control stick, the pilot can alter the pitch of some of the blades more than others. The stick will increase the pitch of the blades moving away from the direction the pilot wants to travel and decrease the pitch of the blades advancing towards it. This produces unequal lift, which tilts the rotor in the direction of travel. In this way, the pilot can make the helicopter move forwards, backward, or sideways.

Flying a helicopter becomes even more complicated when the pilot wants to fly forward *and* upwards!

Helicopters at Work

Although helicopters have been used mostly for military purposes, they have also done a wide range of non-military jobs.

Agriculture

With their slow-flying speed and rotor downwash, helicopters soon proved they were ideal for crop-dusting and crop-spraying. In 1948, for example, Bell 47s helped fight the annual locust plague in Argentina and saved crops worth millions of dollars. Since then, helicopters have become an essential tool of agriculture.

Oil Industry

The offshore oil industry is almost wholly dependent on helicopters to service its rigs and drilling platforms. All kinds of helicopters have been used for this work, including the Boeing-Vertol commercial Chinook and the Aerospatiale Puma.

Survey

Helicopters are used to check power lines for breaks and oil and gas pipelines for leaks. They can even carry out seismic surveys in inaccessible areas, to investigate the chances of possible earthquakes.

Police

Many police forces throughout the world operate their own helicopters. Even the Texas Ranger has traded his horse for a helicopter! Equipped with "heli-tele" cameras, police helicopters can keep an eye on traffic conditions, carry out crowd surveillance, and search for missing persons.

Helicopters for Business

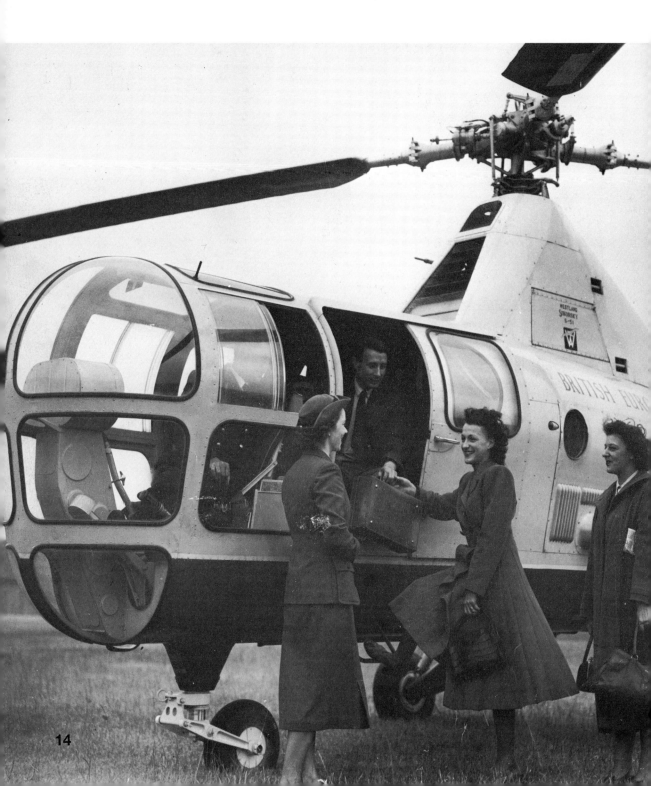

Helicopter airlines:

Helicopters have never been able to compete with airplanes in medium- or long-range passenger transport. But they have been successful on short trips, particularly from airports to city centers, where they can make use of "pinnacle heliports" on top of tall buildings.

The early development of helicopter airlines was linked closely with the award of air mail services to the airlines. Los Angeles Airways began the world's first scheduled helicopter service on October 1, 1947, when it won a three year contract to carry the U.S. mail. The next year British European Airways began the first helicopter air mail service in the U.K., followed in 1949 by a scheduled night time passenger service.

Executive helicopters:

The helicopter has been successful as a craft for businessmen who are in a hurry. Most major cities operate helicopter services, which take executives to airports. Many large corporations own their own helicopters.

One of the most famous helicopters used for executive purposes is the Bell JetRanger, originally flown in 1962. The JetRanger III made helicopter history when the Australian Dick Smith flew his craft *Australian Explorer* around the world between August 5, 1982, and July 22, 1983, covering 35,258 miles (56,742 kilometers). This was the first ever solo helicopter flight around the globe.

Helicopters got their first real chance to show what they could do in the Korean War in 1950. They could put down and pick up men in places no other forms of transport could reach.

Helicopters could rush the wounded back to medical army surgical hospitals (MASH) on stretchers mounted either side. "Korean Angels," as the helicopters were nicknamed, reduced the death rate from wounds to the lowest in the history of war.

Impressed by their performance, the U.S. Army ordered larger transport helicopters, like the Boeing-Vertol CH-113 Labrador and the CH-47 Chinook. These giants could carry up to 44 soldiers to and from the battlefield. In an emergency, they could carry more. During the Vietnam war, a Chinook evacuated 147 refugees and their possessions in one trip.

The Chinook can also carry heavy equipment such as jeeps, field guns and trucks. Helicopters of this type recovered more than 11,000 wrecked aircraft during the Vietnam War.

The flying banana:

One of the earliest, and ugliest, troop carrying helicopters was the Piasecki HRP-1, nicknamed "the flying banana." This craft, which first flew in the early 1950s, enabled the U.S. Army to airlift large numbers of troops into combat areas.

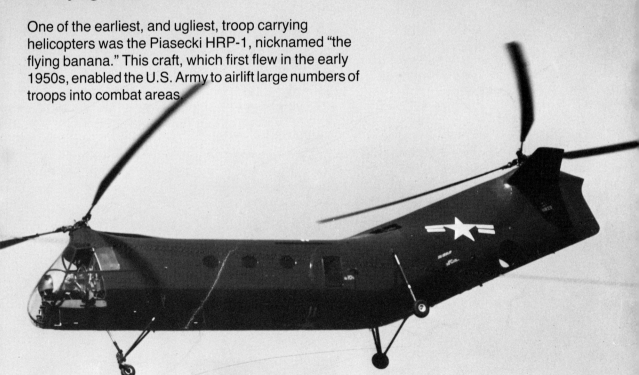

Fighting Helicopters

In war, the slow speed of helicopters makes them vulnerable to attack from the ground. The U.S. Army soon realized that, if helicopters were to survive, they would have to be armed and protected with armor-plating. They would also have to be able to fly faster.

This led to the development of the "gunship," the helicopter that could fight back. The gunship was followed by the attack helicopter, a fast, heavily armed machine designed to hunt and destroy enemy tanks and installations. Attack helicopters can also act as armed escorts for transport helicopters.

The first attack helicopter built solely for that purpose was the Bell Model 207 Sioux Scout. However, this helicopter has side-by-side seating in the cockpit, and its width made it vulnerable to ground fire. Bell therefore developed tandem seating, with one pilot behind the other, for the Model 209 HueyCobra. This narrowed the fuselage to a width of three feet.

The HueyCobra went into service in 1967 and became the most famous – and feared – helicopter of the Vietnam war. It had a top speed of 219 miles per hour (352 kilometers per hour). Over 1,000 machines were built within a few years.

The modern successor to the Bell HueyCobra is the Hughes YAH 64 Apache. This is slower than its predecessor but more heavily armed. Its arsenal includes 1,200 rounds of cannon shells, 76 rockets and 16 anti-tank missiles. The first Apaches were delivered to the U.S. Army in 1984.

Unusual Helicopters

The history of vertical flight is full of unusual craft. Some never got off the ground. Others were highly successful. Yet, because of their odd appearance, perhaps, they were never put into production.

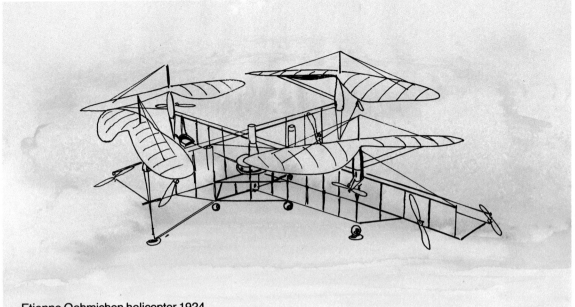

Etienne Oehmichen helicopter 1924.

The portable helicopter

In the late 1950s, Hiller, an American helicopter manufacturer, produced the Rotorcycle, a one-man helicopter that could be folded up like a tent. A man could assemble the Rotorcycle and fly it in under five minutes!

It was built for the U.S. Navy as an observation helicopter, and was highly successful. It had a top speed of 70 miles per hour (113 kilometers an hour). Yet it was never produced in large numbers.

The flying platform

Another unusual helicopter was the Lackner DH-4 Aerocycle, first flown in 1955. In this craft, the pilot stood upright on a small circular platform while two rotors whirled beneath his feet. A small engine mounted on the platform drove the Aerocycle at speeds of up to 75 miles per hour (121 kilometers an hour). The Aerocycle was built for the U.S. Army, and soldiers learned how to handle it in just 20 minutes!

1963 helicopter designed by Ray Cargill, controlled by an overhead stick and foot operated rudders. Top speed 100 mph. It could climb to 1,500 feet and fly 100 miles on 6 gallons of fuel.

The autogyro that became a star

An autogyro called Little Nellie became the star of the James Bond film, *You Only Live Twice*. The craft was designed, built, and flown by Wing Commander K. H. Wallis. It engaged in an air-to-air battle, complete with missiles, in the film.

Wallis autogyros have done more serious work, carrying out coastal ecology surveys and detecting leaks in buried water pipes. They have also helped in the search for the Loch Ness monster in Scotland!

Convertiplanes

In the 1950s and 1960s odd looking aircraft appeared that were a mixture of helicopter and autogyro. They were known as "convertiplanes."

Convertiplanes caught the imagination of aircraft designers because they combined the simplicity and cheapness of operation of the autogyro in forward flight and the maneuverability of the helicopter in horizontal flight.

The first successful convertiplane was the British Fairey Rotodyne, which made its maiden flight in 1957. The Rotodyne had four jets on the tips of its rotor blades that drove them around like a helicopter rotor. Once the craft had risen from the ground, the tip jets were switched off and two forward-facing engines mounted on the aircraft's wings took over. The engines drove it forward through the air like an airplane. Lift was provided by the rotor blades, which spun freely like the blades of an autogyro.

On January 5, 1959, the Fairey Rotodyne flew at 190.9 miles per hour (307.22 kilometers per hour) over a 60 mile closed circuit. This is still a record for convertiplanes. However, rising costs led to the cancellation of Rotodyne in 1962.

Other countries also built convertiplanes. The Soviet Union's Vintokryl was similar to the Rotodyne. It made its first (and last) appearance in 1961. Since then, experiments have continued, but no convertiplanes have gone into commercial or military service.

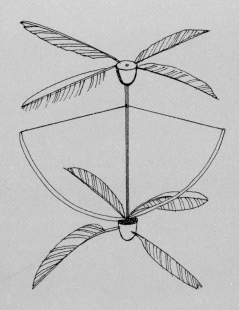

Cayley's model helicopter 1796.

The first convertiplane?

An English baronet, Sir George Cayley, designed what may have been the first convertiplane in the early 19th century. It had two propellers for forward propulsion and four rotors for vertical propulsion. The four-bladed rotors were made from bird feathers!

Below: A model of Cayley's convertiplane 1843.

Giant Helicopters

Helicopters can handle heavy work, transporting large loads over long distances. In 1985, Russian helicopters dropped a total of 5,000 tons of sand, clay, dolomite, and lead on the damaged nuclear reactor at Chernobyl.

Some of the largest helicopters ever seen have been built to do this work. The first heavyweight helicopter was the Cierva W-11 Air Horse, built in 1948. It had three rotors, each 47 feet in diameter, and could lift 14,000 pounds (6,300 kg). However, both prototypes developed faults, and the design was abandoned.

The most successful of the giants was the Sikorsky S-64 Skycrane, which first flew in 1962. It was designed to carry huge containers, which were tucked into its body. In the Vietnam war, it could lift whole aircraft, and was used to salvage damaged planes. In commercial use, it could transport whole prefabricated buildings.

The largest rotor of any helicopter ever built belonged to the American Hughes XH-17. This monster, built in the 1950s, had a rotor diameter of 130 feet (37.62 meters) and was so large that it could straddle two automobiles with its wheels.

The largest rotary wing aircraft ever flown was the Soviet Union's Mil V-12. At the Paris Air Show in 1969, the three-rotor V-12 lifted a load of 88,636 pounds (40,204.5 kg) to a height of 7,398 feet (2,255 meters). This immense load – nearly 40 tons – was almost twice the take off weight of the Skycrane.

The Mil V-12 has now been abandoned. Currently, the world's largest helicopter is the Soviet Mil Mi-26. This single-rotor craft can lift 44,090 pounds (20,000 kg) – equal to the load of a Lockheed C-130 Hercules transport aircraft – and can accommodate more than 100 people.

The largest helicopter outside the Soviet Union is the Sikorsky Super Stallion.

Sikorsky S-60

Sikorsky Super Stallion

The future of the giants

Although giant helicopters have proved their usefulness, there is a limit to how they can grow. The larger the rotors, the greater the problem of vibration becomes. Helicopters of the future may have tip jets on their blades to control vibration.

Helicopters to the Rescue

Re-fuelling in mid air.

Igor Sikorsky, father of the helicopter, hoped that helicopters would help rather than hurt mankind. In their role as rescuers, they have. Helicopters have plucked people from places which no one could reach.

In 1958, a helicopter rescued two air traffic controllers who were trapped on the rooftop of the control tower at Brussels International Airport, which had caught fire. This was the first of many helicopter rescues from blazing buildings.

Helicopters have also played a vital part in mountain rescue operations. The Garde Aerienne Suisse de Sauvetage, an Alpine lifesaving service supported by voluntary contributions, uses small helicopters to rescue stranded climbers. The task is dangerous, since freak winds and down drafts can dash a helicopter against the mountainside.

Helicopters also assist the Coast Guard in sea rescue. Although a helicopter cannot take off in winds stronger than 40 knots, once it is in the air, it can stay there, however bad the weather.

Occasionally, helicopters have saved the lives of whole communities. In the floods that marooned millions of people in Bangladesh in 1970, helicopters ferried in thousands of tons of food and medicine. Nobody else could reach them.

Helicopters at Sea

Helicopters act as the eyes and ears of modern warships. It is their job to look and listen for enemy warships and submarines.

Because a helicopter hovers high above a warship, its radar can scan much farther than the ship's. Similarly, by dipping a sonar device deep in the water, a helicopter can detect the sounds of a submarine that a ship's sonar might miss.

Helicopters can attack as well as defend warships. Attack helicopters like the French Super Puma are armed with Exocets, long-range missiles that can destroy a warship with one hit. Others carry depth bombs for attacking submarines.

Transport helicopters, like the Chinook, are used to transfer men and equipment from one ship to another. They are also used to rescue pilots who have been forced to ditch their aircraft and eject into the sea.

Helicopters played a key role in the Falklands war in 1982. On the first day of the British landing on the islands, seven Sea Kings lifted almost a million pounds of equipment and over 520 troops. Sea Kings also had the unnerving task of acting as decoys to deflect any attacking missiles from the warships.

The Rope of Rescue

Helicopters do not have to land to rescue people in trouble. They can hover overhead and winch them to safety by means of a cable.

The first air–sea rescue using a winch happened off Long island Sound in 1945. Two men were winched up from a tanker that was stranded on a reef in gale force winds. When an American Air Rescue helicopter saved 14 Japanese seamen in the same way in 1955, the Japanese dubbed the winch recovery "the rope of rescue."

Different countries have developed different kinds of winches. In Britain, Lieutenant Commander John Sproule invented a device which could scoop an unconscious person from the sea: a pocket-shaped net that the helicopter trails slowly across the surface of the water. United States Coast Guard helicopters trawl for victims with a basket-shaped net called the "Billy Pugh." During the U.S. space program, Coast Guard helicopters used this method to recover astronauts from the sea.

Thousands of people each year owe their lives to the "rope of rescue."

How a winch and cable works

The Sea King helicopter, a derivative of the Sikorsky S-61, is used for SAR (search and rescue). It has a crew of four: a pilot, co-pilot, radar operator, and winchman. The helicopter is fitted with a flight control system that allows it to hover automatically in bad weather and at night. Using this system, the winchman can maneuver the helicopter by remote control from his position in the cabin doorway.

The winch cable of a Sea King is 240 feet long and can be released at 200 feet a minute. It has a breaking point of 3,000 pounds, but it is only ever used to the maximum of 600 pounds – the weight of three heavy people.

Faster Helicopters

Helicopters cannot normally fly very fast because their rotating blades have a lower "angle of attack" when they are advancing through the air than when they are retreating. (The angle of attack is the angle at which a blade or wing is set to give an aircraft lift.)

If the advancing and retreating blades operated at the same angle, they would give more lift on one side of the helicopter than the other, and the helicopter would turn over.

This is why helicopters can never fly as fast as airplanes. However powerful their engines are, their speed will always be limited by their blades.

One answer is to design a blade that moves through the air without creating shock waves. Westland, the British helicopter manufacturers have recently invented a paddle shaped rotor blade that does this. The swept tip enables the blade to cut through the advancing air at more than the speed of sound.

With the new blade, helicopters can carry heavier weights. They can also fly faster. In August 1986, a Westland Lynx helicopter was flown at 249.1 miles an hour, beating the previous record of 228 miles per hour held by a Soviet Mi-24 helicopter since 1978.

The Most Successful Helicopter in the World

The helicopter that ranks as the most successful in the world is the Bell Model 47. This model was in continuous production from 1946 to 1967. With its familiar "goldfish bowl" canopy, it became the best known helicopter of them all.

The Bell 47 was designed by Lawrence D. Bell, founder of the Bell Aircraft Corporation. In 1943, Bell built the Model 30, a two seater prototype. This led to the Model 47 a few years later.

The Bell 47 achieved a string of "firsts." It was awarded the first commercial license in the United States and the first Type Approval Certificate for a commercial helicopter anywhere in the world.

It was also the first helicopter licensed in the United States for crop-dusting and was probably the first helicopter to be used by the oil industry.

In 1947, Bell 47s were used for the first helicopter air mail service in continental Europe.

However, its greatest achievement was military. During the Korean War, helicopters airlifted more than 23,000 United Nations casualties to field hospitals. Some 18,000 of these were carried by Bell 47s. As a result the Bell 47 was nicknamed the "Korean Angel."

Production of the Bell 47 for U.S. forces ended in 1968, and all production in the United States ended in 1974. But the Bell 47 continued to be manufactured in other countries until 1976, setting a record for production that has never been equaled.

Home-Built Helicopters

Once rotary winged aircraft had been accepted by the professionals, some manufacturers began to offer them to the amateurs – the people who fly for fun.

These manufacturers designed aircraft that could be built at home, either from a plan or with a kit of parts. Home built craft have introduced thousands of people to the thrills of rotary winged flight.

The cheapest and simplest rotary winged aircraft to build at home is the autogyro. The popularity of this craft among amateur flyers is largely due to Igor Bensen, who began selling plans and kits for his Gyro-Copter in the mid-1950s. The Gyro-Copter is powered by a 40-horsepower engine. It has a top speed of 85 miles per hour (137 kilometers per hour) and can fly 100 miles (160 kilometers) on six U.S. gallons (22.75 liters). More than 10,000 plans for the Gyro-Copter have been sold.

Assembling a helicopter at home requires more skill and more money. One of the first helicopters for amateurs was the Adams-Wilson XH1, which first flew in 1958. Like the autogyro, this was powered by a 40-horsepower motorcycle engine.

G-AV YW

Today, one of the best known manufacturers of home built helicopters is Rotor Way Aircraft Incorporated of Arizona. Their helicopters have 145 horsepower engines and can fly at 112 miles per hour (180 kilometers per hour).

The Helicopters of the Future

Bell is now developing a larger tilt rotor aircraft for military use. This could be used, for example, for a Marine assault mission, where troops have to be transported at speed and landed in rough country. Known as the V-22 Osprey, the aircraft will have a cruising speed of 300 knots.

However useful helicopters have proved to be, they are still slow and expensive to operate. If helicopters are to develop in the future, they must overcome these problems.

One promising solution is the tilt-rotor. This combines the speed and performance of an airplane with the maneuverability of a helicopter. The theory of the tilt rotor is simple. When the rotor blades are tilted upwards, the craft rises vertically. When they are tilted forward, the craft moves forward.

Bell has developed a tilt rotor aircraft, called the SV-15. This has an ordinary airplane fuselage, with two tilting turboprop engines at the tips of the wings. These are fitted with rotor blades 35 feet (7.62 meters) in diameter. Conversion from one mode of flight to another takes just 12 seconds. This arrangement gives the XV-15 twice the speed and range of conventional helicopters.

Above: Three view drawing of Osprey V-22.

Below: Tilt Rotor.

Helicopter Records

The largest helicopter

The Mil Mi-26, built in the Soviet Union is currently the world's largest helicopter.

The fastest helicopter

The Lynx, built in Britain, pushed the world speed record for helicopters to 249.1 miles an hour in August 1986, using redesigned rotors.

The first non-stop Atlantic crossing by helicopter

Two Sikorsky HH-3Es, built in the United States, and nicknamed Jolly Green Giants, made the first non-stop crossing of the Atlantic by helicopters between May 31 and June 1, 1967.

The highest helicopter

The Lama, built in France, took the world altitude record for helicopters to 40,820 feet (12,442 meters) in 1972.

First helicopter flight around the world

Americans Ross Perot, Jr. and Jay W. Coburn completed the very first helicopter flight around the world in their Long Ranger II, *The Spirit of Texas*, on September 30, 1982. The 29-stage flight had begun on September 1.

First landing on a building

A Kellett KD-1 autogyro made the first aircraft landing on the roof of a building during an experimental air mail service to mark the opening of the Philadelphia Post Office in 1935.

First solo helicopter flight around the world

Australian Dick Smith flew a Bell JetRanger III, *Australian Explorer*, solo around the world between August 5, 1982, and July 22, 1983, a distance of 35,258 miles (56,742 kilometers).

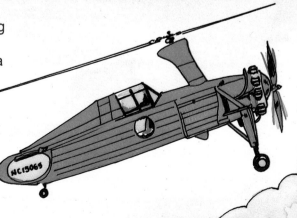

Glossary

Angle of Attack   The angle at which the blade of a helicopter meets the flow of air. Increasing the angle of attack causes the helicopter to climb. Decreasing the angle makes it descend.

Autogyro   A rotary-winged aircraft in which the rotor spins freely (freewheels). The forward thrust of a autogyro is provided by a propeller or jet.

Chopper   Nickname for a helicopter. It refers to the fact that a helicopter could chop off the head of someone who forgot to duck beneath the blades!

Convertiplane   An aircraft which can be flown either as a helicopter or as an autogyro.

Cyclic pitch control   A system which enables the pilot to change direction of a helicopter's flight. The *collective pitch lever* controls vertical movement.

Disymmetry of lift   Unequal forces acting on the advancing and retreating blades of a helicopter. In modern helicopters, blades are fitted to an articulated hub to overcome this problem.

Rotor   Short for "rotator" or rotating wing. The rotating blades of a helicopter which enable it to fly.

Torque   A reaction in the opposite direction of a rotor, which turns a helicopter on its side. This can be corrected by a smaller, vertical rotor on the tail of the helicopter.

VTOL   The initials stand for Vertical Take-Off and Landing.

STOL   Denotes an aircraft capable of Short Take-Off and Landing.

Index

Acknowledgements

We would like to thank and acknowledge the following people for the use of their photographs and transparancies.

p. 6/7   Bell Helicopter Textron Inc.

p. 8/8   Topham Picture Library.

p. 10/11   Bell Helicopter Textron Inc.

p. 12/13   Metropolitan Police
            Shell Photo Service

p. 14/15   Topham Picture Library
            Bell Helicopter Textron Inc.

p. 16/17   Topham Picture Library

p. 18/19   Bell Helicopter Textron Inc.
            Sigma Projects Ltd.

p. 22/23   Photographs Courtesy of Commander K. H.
            Wallis

p. 26/27   Sigma Projects Ltd.
            Topham Picture Library

p. 28/29   Sigma Projects Ltd.

p. 30/31   Sigma Projects Ltd.
            Topham Picture Library

p. 32/33   Sigma Projects Ltd.

p. 34/35   Sigma Projects Ltd.

p. 36/37   Sigma Projects Ltd.

p. 38/39   Topham Picture Library

p. 40/41   Bell Helicopter Textron Inc.
            Sigma Projects Ltd.

p. 42/43   Sigma Projects Ltd.

Cover photographs:
  Sigma Projects Ltd.
  Shell Photo Service
  Chris Gilbert

Frontispiece: Metropolitan Police

Arwork by: Sharon Perks

Design and Production by: Suzie Home